M000220014

GALE
CENGAGE Learning

Novels for Students, Volume 1

and other applicable laws. The authors and editors of this work have added value to the underlying factual material herein through one or more of the following: unique and original selection, coordination, expression, arrangement, and classification of the information.

All rights to this publication will be vigorously defended.

Copyright © 1997
Gale Research
835 Penobscot Building
645 Griswold St.
Detroit, Ml 48226-4094

This book is printed on acid-free paper that meets the minimum requirements of American National Standard for Information Sciences—Permanence Paper for Printed Library Materials, ANSI Z39.48-1984.

ISBN 0-7876-1686-9
ISSN 1094-3552

Printed in the United States of America
10 9 8 7 6 5

The Bell Jar

Sylvia Plath

1963

Introduction

The Bell Jar was published in London, England, in January 1963, less than one month before its author, Sylvia Plath, committed suicide by asphyxiation. Published under the pseudonym of Victoria Lucas, the novel opened to some positive reviews, although Plath was distressed by its reception. In 1966, *The Bell Jar* was published in England under Plath's real name. By the early 1970s, it had been published to many favorable reviews in the United States.

The short, heavily autobiographical novel

details six months in the life of its protagonist, Esther Greenwood. In the narrative's opening chapter, Esther, an overachieving college student in 1953, is spending an unhappy summer as a guest editor for a fashion magazine in New York City. After her internship ends, she returns home to live with her mother, grows increasingly depressed, suffers a mental breakdown and attempts suicide, and is institutionalized. By the book's conclusion, the hospital is about to release a somewhat improved Esther to the "real world."

The Bell Jar functions on many literary levels, but it is perhaps most obviously about the limitations imposed on young, intelligent American women in the 1950s. A brilliant woman with literary aspirations, Esther peers into the future and does not like her choices. She can learn shorthand—as her mother strongly encourages—and land some menial office job after college, or she can marry, live in suburbia, and nurture her husband. What she really wants to do—make a living as a writer—seems unlikely, especially in a profession with so few feminine role models.

Also complicating her situation, Esther, a student on a full-time scholarship, is surrounded by people from families much wealthier than her own; not having the financial resources of her peers further limits her choices.

As we understand today, *The Bell Jar* relies heavily on Plath's own life experience. Like Esther, Plath attended Smith College on scholarship, earned top grades, published poetry at a young age, and majored in English. Like Esther, she did a summer internship in New York City, suffered a mental collapse, and was institutionalized. Both eventually recovered to the extent they were released from psychiatric units into the "real world." While Esther's future, by the novel's conclusion, remains uncertain, Sylvia Plath's recovery only lasted a decade: On February 11, 1963, she elected to end her own life.

Author Biography

Remembered today for her horrifying death as well as for her impressive body of literature, Sylvia Plath was born on 27 October 1932 in Jamaica Plain, Massachusetts, to Aurelia Schober and Otto Emil Plath. In 1940, her father, a professor of entomology, died, an event that left lasting psychological scars on Plath. References to her dead father permeate Plath's work, including *The Colossus* and *The Bell Jar.*

In 1942, Aurelia Plath found work teaching in a medical/secretarial program at Boston University. The family settled in Wellesley, Massachusetts. An excellent student, Plath showed enormous determination to get her fiction published. She submitted forty-five pieces to the magazine *Seventeen* before they published her story, "And Summer Will Not Come Again" in 1950.

At Smith College, she wrote poetry, was elected to various class offices, and received prizes for both her prose and poetry. That this gifted woman had many insecurities is obvious in one of her letters to a friend, which reveals "for the few little outward successes I may seem to have, there are acres of misgivings and self-doubts." Part of Plath's frustration lay in what she perceived as a choice between becoming a free-spirited poet or choosing the wife/mother alternative.

In the summer of 1952, she was chosen as a

guest editor in *Mademoiselle's* College Board Contest. The prize, a month of employment at the magazine in New York City, did not elevate Plath's mood. Despite the numerous frills her expense account afforded her—living at the Barbizon Hotel, expensive meals, meeting celebrities—Plath found the overall experience to be artificial. Her general disillusionment, dating experiences, and interactions with her boss and co-workers figure prominently into the first half of *The Bell Jar*.

Plath returned home after her employment ended and learned that she did not get accepted into the summer writing course that she had counted on. Her miserable subsequent months—including confused attempts to establish her career goals, a highly publicized suicide attempt, electroshock therapy, institutionalization, and recovery—are apparent in the second half of *The Bell Jar*.

Plath returned to Smith College in January 1954, graduated *summa cum laude* in June 1955, and won a Fulbright fellowship to study at Cambridge University in England. There, she met aspiring poet Ted Hughes, to whom she was immediately attracted. They married in June 1956. In 1957, the couple left England and settled in Northampton, Massachusetts, where Plath taught freshman English at Smith College. Considered an outstanding instructor, Plath also wrote poetry and worked on a preliminary draft of *The Bell Jar*.

In 1959, she and her husband returned to England; in 1960 her collection of poetry *The Colossus* was published by William Heinemann. Its initial reviews were not encouraging, although certain critics praised Plath's gifts for language. In April, 1960, she gave birth to a daughter, Frieda.

For the next year, Plath did not write much. A busy wife and mother, her health was poor, having suffered a miscarriage and an appendectomy. However, by spring 1961, she was working on *The Bell Jar*. She applied for and received a Saxon fellowship. In February, 1962, she gave birth to a son, Nicholas.

By summer 1962, her marriage to Ted Hughes was dissolving. He left Plath and their children; a devastated Plath now wrote poems at a phenomenal rate, sometimes one a day. *The Bell Jar* was published in January, 1963.

Although generally depressed in the last year of her life, Plath had one joyous experience. In December, 1962, she and her children moved into a flat in which the poet William Butler Yeats had once lived. But with her poor health, the rigors of raising two children by herself, and not having received the critical acclaim she desired, Plath ended her life in February, 1963.

Since her death, Plath's reputation as a writer and a cult figure has grown, and much of her work has been issued posthumously. More than thirty years after her death, Plath biographies are published with almost clock-like regularity, and critics still analyze her most famous poetry, as well as her more obscure work.

New York: Chapters 1-9

Sylvia Plath's fictionalized autobiography, *The Bell Jar*, records seven months in the life of Esther Greenwood. In the summer of 1953, Esther has just finished her junior year in college. She is working in New York City as a writing intern at a fashion magazine. It is June, the same month in which Julius and Ethel Rosenberg are executed by electrocution. The Rosenbergs had been convicted of treason for allegedly selling atomic secrets to the Soviet Union (as it was then called). Esther lives at the Amazon hotel for women with other magazine interns, including Doreen. Her sarcastic remarks on the other women's primness echo Esther's own feelings. Though successful and intelligent, Esther begins to doubt her own abilities to continue performing at such a high level. Her depression deepens as the summer progresses.

Esther and Doreen skip a party sponsored by the magazine, going out instead with Lenny Shepherd, a disc jockey, and his friend. Esther introduces herself as Elly Higginbottom from Chicago, in order to disassociate herself from the experience. She leaves Doreen at Lenny's apartment and returns to the Amazon. Doreen returns much later, drunk and knocking on Esther's door.

One morning, Esther muses on her

depressioninduced inertia: "I wondered why I couldn't go the whole way doing what I should any more. This made me sad and tired. Then I wondered why I couldn't go the whole way doing what I shouldn't, the way Doreen did, and this made me even sadder and more tired." Then her boss, Jay Cee, calls Esther into the office, concerned about her waning enthusiasm for her work. Esther tries to reassure Jay Cee, not revealing that she feels two conflicting pressures. On the one hand, she has a desire for a writing career. On the other hand, she feels that social norms are pushing her toward the more practical pursuits of shorthand and motherhood. At a luncheon sponsored by *Ladies' Day* magazine, Esther indulges in the grand spread of delicacies while she entertains memories of her own less privileged life. All the women who attend the luncheon later suffer from acute food poisoning.

Esther recalls her past relationship with Buddy Willard, a boy from her hometown who is now a medical student at Yale. Buddy visits Esther's college to go to a dance with Joan Gilling, a student there and a girl from Buddy's and Esther's town. Before the dance, however, he asks Esther for a date and later they begin regularly seeing each other. During one of the following summers, Buddy sleeps with a woman with whom he works. Esther learns of his infidelity to her just before he contracts tuberculosis and enters a sanatorium. Esther determines to avenge herself and assert her independence by sleeping with a man. When in New York, she goes on a date with a man named Constantin, but nothing happens.

As Esther waits to have her photograph taken for the magazine, she feels her sadness and uncertainty welling up. She is called to pose and she recalls:

> When they asked me what I wanted
> to be I said I didn't know.

"Oh, sure you know," the photographer said.

"She wants," said Jay Cee wittily, "to be everything."

I said I wanted to be a poet.

Then they scouted about for something for me to hold.

Jay Cee suggested a book of poems, but the photographer said no, that was too obvious. It should be something that showed what inspired the poems. Finally Jay Cee unclipped the single, long-stemmed paper rose from her latest hat.

The photographer fiddled with his hot white lights. "Show us how happy it makes you to write a poem."

Though Esther tries obediently to smile, she bursts into tears before the photograph is taken. On her last night in New York, she accompanies Doreen to a country club dance where Esther is nearly raped by a rich man named Marco.

Suburban Boston: Chapters 10-13

In July, Esther returns to her mother's home in

suburban Boston and becomes increasingly depressed. Having been denied admission to a writing course she had planned to take, she cannot decide what to do instead. For several weeks, she does not shower and is unable to read or write. She develops insomnia. On the urging of her mother, Esther sees a psychiatrist, Dr. Gordon. After one electroconvulsive therapy session, Esther becomes more and more suicidal, poring over reports of suicides in the tabloids and considering various methods of self-slaughter.

After a failed attempt to work as a hospital candystriper, Esther visits her father's grave and grieves for him for the first time in her life. Having spent the last of her savings, she determines to act on her suicidal impulses. She descends into the cellar of her mother's house, conceals herself in a remote crevice, and swallows fifty sleeping pills.

Hospitalization: Chapters 14-18

Esther, lying partially blinded in a suburban hospital, fades in and out of a coma. She is transferred to a psychiatric ward in a Boston hospital. Philomena Guinea, who had endowed the scholarship which enabled Esther to attend college, learns of Esther's situation and removes her to a private hospital in the country. Mrs. Guinea, a writer of popular novels, only intervenes because Esther's mother assures her that the root cause of Esther's suicide attempt is not emotional distress over a boy but over her writing.

At the private hospital, Esther's depression is still profound but she is intrigued by Dr. Nolan: "I didn't think they had woman psychiatrists." Though Dr. Nolan promises Esther that she will not be subject to the kind of electroconvulsive treatment she received at Dr. Gordon's clinic, Esther is still wary.

Joan Gilling, Esther's college acquaintance who sporadically dated Buddy Willard, arrives at the hospital. She shows Esther some newspaper clippings that describe the police and her mother searching for and eventually finding the comatose Esther. The nurses give her regular insulin injections. She suffers insulin shock (which is intended to serve the same purpose as electroconvulsive therapy) and is revived with glucose treatment. Esther's mother brings her roses for her birthday, which Esther throws in the wastebasket. After that visit, Dr. Nolan informs her that she will no longer have to receive visitors, which pleases Esther.

As Esther improves, she moves to another unit in which the most stable patients live. Esther again undergoes electroconvulsive therapy, which she finds slightly less painful than her previous experience. Both Esther and Joan receive letters from Buddy Willard. Joan confesses that she has never had romantic feelings for Buddy, but that she "likes" Esther. Esther, who had accidentally discovered Joan in bed with another woman patient, rebuffs her advances.

Esther tells Dr. Nolan that she feels

constrained by the thought that she will have to sacrifice her career if she were to marry and have children. The doctor arranges for Esther to be fitted with a diaphragm, which, like all birth control devices, was illegal in Massachusetts at that time. Esther feels enormously liberated.

The Bell Jar Suspended: Chapters 19-20

Esther, all but cleared to be discharged from the hospital, determines to return to college for the winter term. She lives at the hospital while she waits for the beginning of the semester, having been discouraged from living with her mother. While on a pass, she meets a young Harvard professor named Irwin. She has sex for the first time in her life with him and afterward bleeds profusely. Irwin drives Esther to the Cambridge house in which Joan has been living since her recent release from the psychiatric hospital. Joan, alarmed by Esther's hemorrhaging, takes her to the emergency room. Soon after this incident, Joan returns to the psychiatric hospital and subsequently hangs herself.

After a great snowstorm, Buddy Willard visits Esther at the hospital and she relieves him of the guilt he feels over her hospitalization and Joan's suicide. She also severs her ties with Irwin and then with Joan by attending her funeral. Just as Esther is trying to devise a proper ritual "for being born twice —patched, retreaded and approved for the road," she is called into a meeting of doctors who will, she hopes, authorize her release.

Characters

Betsy

One of the guest interns at *Ladies' Day*, Betsy represents the ultimate "nice girl": an All-American girl from Kansas who will wait patiently for a husband, a big farm, and plenty of children—without losing her virginity before marriage. In *The Bell Jar*, Betsy attempts to keep Esther away from Doreen's vampish influence, and for a while Esther seems receptive. Ultimately, however, Esther cannot accept the simple naivete of Betsy, whom she comes to see as the "Pollyanna Cowgirl."

Cal

Esther's date at the beach. Like many of the men in the novel, Cal attempts to teach Esther something, in his case, the methods of suicide.

Constantin

A translator at the United Nations. Originally, Esther attempts to get him to seduce her. Unfortunately, when they actually go to bed, he simply falls asleep beside her. In the novel, he is treated as one more member of the patriarchy that ultimately disappoints Esther.

physicians. Contrast this to the earlier Esther who once threw her clothes out of a New York hotel window, ate raw meat, made an unsuccessful suicide attempt, and often stared catatonically into space.

Mrs. Greenwood

Esther Greenwood's widowed mother, Mrs. Greenwood appears periodically throughout the narrative. Although she seldom articulates it, Esther harbors great hostility toward her mother, as evidenced in the following passage: "I had always been my father's favorite, and it seemed fitting that I should take on a mourning my mother had never bothered with." A teacher of secretarial students, Mrs. Greenwood wants her daughter to learn shorthand so she will have a job after college. She does little to encourage Esther's literary aspirations. For example, after Esther returns from New York City to move back with her mother, Mrs. Greenwood unsympathetically passes on this bad news: "I think I should tell you right away, you didn't make the writing course."

Philomena Guinea

A famous and successful writer, she is also the woman who sponsors Esther's scholarship. She agrees to subsidize Esther's stay at a posh psychiatric hospital as soon as she learns Esther is not pregnant.

Elly Higginbottom

See Esther Greenwood

Hilda

Like Esther, she is a guest editor at *Ladies' Day*. A designer of hats and other accessories, she demonstrates no curiosity or any positive emotion in the brief period that Esther spends with her.

Irwin

The man to whom Esther loses her virginity. Described by Esther as "rather ugly and bespectacled," she does not have romantic feelings for him and is simply tired of being a virgin.

Jay Cee

Esther's boss at *Ladies' Day*, Jay Cee is an unglamorous, savvy editor, something of a rarity in a profession dominated by men in the 1950s. Although perceived by the summer interns as intimidating, Jay Cee does show some genuine concern for Esther by directly asking what her future plans are and by making suggestions. Esther's attitude toward her is ambivalent. While she admires Jay Cee's intelligence and claims indifference to her unattractive appearance, Esther also feels Jay Cee and some other women "wanted to teach me something … but I didn't think they had anything to teach me."

Marco

Accurately described by Esther as a "woman-hater," Marco sees women in one of two categories: Madonnas or whores. On his date with Esther, he admits to being in love with his first cousin, who intends to become a nun. Treating Esther like a whore, he gives her a diamond stickpin, throws her in a muddy ditch, and threatens to rape her.

Dr. Nolan

One of the few positive characters in the novel, Dr. Nolan is a direct yet humane psychiatrist—the opposite of Dr. Gordon—who empowers Esther after her breakdown. Through Dr. Nolan's influence, Esther comes to understand her own motivations and reconciles with her anger. Not judgmental, she empowers Esther by not criticizing or analyzing her statement toward her mother: "I hate her." When Joan Gilling commits suicide, Dr. Nolan assures Esther that it is no one's fault, certainly not Esther's. Dr. Nolan is also the first person Esther sees after her electroconvulsive shock treatments and the person who coaches her back into reality.

Mrs. Savage

One of the patients at the mental asylum where Esther is staying. She is a rich, idle woman who has apparently committed herself to shame her family.

Lenny Shepherd

An unscrupulous disk jockey who becomes sexually involved with Doreen and unconsciously intimidates Esther. In observing Doreen and Lenny, Esther becomes less impressed with Doreen as a role model.

Valerie

A lobotomized patient whom Esther meets at the mental asylum.

Mr. Willard

The father of Buddy Willard. Not as pretentious as his son, he is nonetheless in the novel to represent the patriarchy of the 1950s.

Mrs. Willard

The mother of Esther's boyfriend, Buddy Willard. A woman who has decided to live her life through her husband, she serves mostly as a negative role model for Esther.

Buddy Willard

Buddy Willard is Esther's boyfriend and a medical student. Originally, Esther enjoyed what she perceived as Buddy's lack of sexual experience ("… he made me feel I was much more sexy …"); when she learns he was having an affair with a

Dodo Conway

To Esther, the model of fertility: a pregnant mother who already has six children. Although it is implied that Dodo is less than an ideal mother, she is greatly admired in Esther's neighborhood simply for having so many children.

Dee Dee

A patient at the mental asylum where Esther is staying. One of the few females in the novel to demonstrate creativity, she composes a tune on the piano, about which "everybody kept saying she ought to get it published, it would be a hit."

Doreen

One of the guest editors at *Ladies' Day*, Doreen represents "the bad girl" among the group: sexy, vulgar, bored. She serves as a counterpoint to traditional "nice girl" Betsy, and Esther alternately envies both of the girls for their solid identities. Although sophisticated with Esther, Doreen dissolves into a passive sex object with the cowboy disk jockey, Lenny. After Doreen parties too much and passes out in her own vomit, Esther further distances herself from her.

Elaine

See Esther Greenwood

Eric

Esther's friend at college. Esther considers him a probable candidate for abandoning her virginity until he says she reminds him of an older sister.

Joan Gilling

A former rival for Buddy Willard's affections, Joan Gilling is eventually admitted to the same posh mental hospital where Esther is making her recovery. Although one of the novel's major characters, she materializes only toward its conclusion. Joan and Esther represent the two most complex characters in *The Bell Jar* and share many similarities. Both attend a prestigious women's college; both are intelligent, accomplished women; both come from the same hometown and went to the same church; both have suicidal tendencies. Further, both come to despise Buddy Willard for similar reasons. What distinguishes Joan and Esther most obviously is money; Joan comes from a wealthy family, whereas Esther's background is modestly middle class. Hence, Joan takes for granted many things—horseback riding, fancy clothes, private lessons—that Esther must struggle to obtain.

Although on the surface, Joan seems to represent the typical upper-class "Seven Sisters" college girl, she is really not. First, she is a physics major in college—a rather unusual choice for a woman in the 1950s. Second, she is even more nakedly ambitious than Esther and does not feign femininity in situations to please men. For example, on bike trips with Buddy Willard, she does not ask for his help ascending high hills. Third, she is not physically attractive (much to Esther's relief), and some critics have written that Joan's attraction to lesbianism can be interpreted as her realization that no man will desire her.

Like her attitude toward most of the major female characters in the novel, Esther is ambivalent toward Joan. "I looked at Joan. In spite of the creepy feeling, and in spite of the old, ingrained dislike, Joan fascinated me." Esther rebuffs Joan's sexual advances, yet turns to her for help after Esther has a terrifying bleeding experience after her first sexual experience.

After Joan commits suicide by hanging, Dr. Nolan assures Esther that it is not her fault. But some critics have linked her death with Esther's recovery and rebirth. It is also ironic that Joan, with all her social status and economic advantages, destroys herself, while struggling Esther is the survivor.

Dr. Gordon

He is the first psychiatrist to examine Esther after her breakdown. Showing little understanding or concern for her, he administers her electroconvulsive shock treatments without getting a second opinion. He then goes on vacation, referring her to a colleague. Dr. Gordon represents the respectable but artificial side of the medical profession.

Esther Greenwood

The protagonist of *The Bell Jar*, Esther Greenwood is a young, highly intelligent college student who has a breakdown. A woman from a modestly middle-class background, but surrounded by many relatively affluent people, Esther represents on the most obvious level an individual unsure of what she wants. The central conflict concerns marriage and motherhood versus literary ambitions. Given her limited financial reserves, her choice is extremely important.

Her attitude toward the other major female characters in the novel is usually ambivalence. At various points in the novel, she sees Doreen, Betsy, Jay Cee, Joan Gilling, and many others as role models, but they all fail her expectations in different ways. Her feelings toward women shift quite abruptly. For example, soon after she wishes she "had a mother like Jay Cee," the ruthless editor has hurt her by criticizing her lack of ambition. Sexy, uninhibited Doreen seems like a nice contrast to the bland guest editors at *Ladies' Day*, but Esther ultimately tires of her promiscuity. Betsy's niceness and virginity strikes Esther as alternatively a blessing and a curse; Joan's lesbian advances appall Esther, but Esther turns to her in a moment of a medical emergency.

The one female character that Esther is unambivalent toward is her mother, Mrs.

Greenwood. "I hate her" sums up her feelings very well. Two reasons explain Esther's loathing. First, her mother discouraged Esther from mourning over her dead father; second, Esther sees her mother as a woman who sacrificed her will for her husband's career.

Media Adaptations

- The movie *The Bell Jar*, based on Sylvia Plath's autobiographical novel of the same name, was directed by Larry Peerce and starred Marilyn Hassett, Julie Harris, Anne Jackson, and Barbara Barrie. Released by Avco Embassy in 1979, it was neither a critical nor commercial success, in large part because the script does not examine the reasons for Esther Greenwood's depression and mental breakdown.

Esther's attitude toward the male characters in the novel seems less confused. She sees Buddy Willard, Constantin, Cal, Irwin, Eric, Marco, and others in mostly sexual terms, candidates to lose her virginity to or potential husbands. In varying degrees, they are all unsympathetic characters, ranging from the pure misogyny of Marco to Buddy Willard's smug superiority. Soon after her date with Cal, Esther loses all interest in men as potential husbands, although she still aspires to lose her virginity.

Despite her intellect, Esther is an extremely impressionable person. That, early in the novel, she lies about her own name to a virtual stranger indicates what little identity she really has. Even her surname, Greenwood, as Linda Wagner-Martin suggests, "was satisfying for reasons both personal and symbolic, and because the novel moves toward Esther's rebirth, the image of green wood is comforting." By the conclusion of *The Bell Jar*, however, Esther represents a kind of survivor, although the extent of her mental and emotional recovery is debatable. She is more confident and able to make some of her own decisions, as evidenced by her instructing Irwin to pay her emergency room bill. Her feelings toward individuals and events are less confused, more rational: she grieves at Joan's funeral, realizes Buddy Willard is "nothing, but a great amiable boredom" to her, and is understandably apprehensive about her interview with the board of waitress while he was seeing her, she feels disillusioned. For Esther, it is not so much the double standard (i.e, it is okay for a man to have a fling but scandalous for a woman to do so) that upsets her; she now feels inferior to Buddy because she is a virgin and he is not.

Esther is competitive with Buddy in other ways. That he, as a doctor, can give pregnant women a drug to minimize their pain during childbirth upsets Esther. To her, the doctors—all male—are depriving the expectant women of both the trauma and beauty of the birth experience simply to achieve the ends. Hence, she imagines Buddy robbing herself of all bodily forms of pleasure.

Esther's fears aside, Buddy is a rather odious character. He seems far more interested in instructing her on such matters as medicine, science, and skiing than in learning anything from her. Joan Gilling's offhand comment about Buddy ("He thought he knew everything. He thought he knew everything about women.") captures his feelings of superiority very well. When Esther learns Buddy has contracted tuberculosis and will need to spend a year in a sanatorium, her reaction is mostly relief that he will be gone a long time. After learning that Esther has been in a mental hospital, Buddy's reaction is "I wonder who you'll marry now, Esther," implying very few men would find her desirable anymore. In light of his own long period of hospitalization for tuberculosis, the remark shows both his hypocrisy and insensitivity.

Themes

Culture Clash

Unlike most of the women who attended Smith College in 1950s, Esther Greenwood of *The Bell Jar* did not come from a wealthy family. That her family gets by on her mother's earnings as a typing teacher and on Esther's full-time scholarship explains why she does not normally have access to such luxuries as expensive clothes, travel, and summer homes. Hence, Esther is outside of the mainstream social circle at college and will never really fit in unless she marries into it. Aware of this, Esther makes many attempts to connect socially— she dates Buddy Willard mostly because he attends Yale; she baby-sits on Cape Cod to be in close proximity to wealthy people; she shops at expensive clothing stores for items on sale.

To complicate matters further, Esther comes to resent her own financial dependence on her mentor, the wealthy writer Philomena Guinea. Since Esther ultimately needs her patronage for continuing psychological care as well as for education, Esther becomes even more frustrated with her own financial dependence, although she seldom expresses this anger directly.

Yet in other ways, Esther is fairly typical of other Smith students: white, educated, attractive, and studious. That she is socially cut off from women with whom she has so much in common is one of the ironies of *The Bell Jar*.

Sex Roles

Although *The Bell Jar* is partly about the impact of economics on a brilliant student with limited financial reserves, it also concerns sex roles in the 1950s. In that decade, women, generally speaking, did not attend college to ultimately support themselves; they were expected to marry eventually. In the novel, there are three women who have created real identities for themselves separate from the men in their life. The unglamorous editor Jay Cee has succeeded in that, but she has also sacrificed a certain amount of femininity to get there; the writer Philomena Guinea has thrived creatively on her own terms; Esther's psychiatrist, Dr. Nolan, emerges as a caring, competent professional. However, they are exceptions in Esther's frame of reference, as well as in the maledominated 1950s American society. More typical are wisecracking Doreen who depends on men for sex if not necessarily for marriage; traditional Betsy who patiently waits for domesticity; Dodo Conway whom Esther perceives as kind of a baby machine; and Joan Gilling whose combination of ambition and lesbianism have not made her into a happy, functional person. Even widowed Mrs. Greenwood, who earns her own money as a typing teacher, does not encourage her smart daughter to flourish: she prefers that Esther learn shorthand and eventually marry well.

Given these feminine influences, Esther channels much of her energy into men as potential husbands or as a means of losing her virginity. Nearly all of the men fall short, often because Esther resents their attempts to informally teach her something without really listening to her. Even men who are not potential lovers fancy themselves as instructors, for example, the old doctor at the sanatorium who foolishly imparts great knowledge about pilgrims. As *The Bell Jar* progresses, Esther loses most of her interest in marriage, but not in losing her virginity.

Esther also reserves much of her affection for her late father, who died when she was only nine, an event from which she has never psychologically recovered. As Lindsay Wagner-Martin wrote in *The Bell Jar: A Novel of the Fifties*, "… while it is—as she has consistently been taught—unseemly for her to be angry with her dead father, there is little stigma attached to her being angry with her living mother."

Search for Self

In *The Bell Jar*, Esther searches consistently for some kind of identity but finds her options limited as a young woman with little money of her own. After a disappointing summer as a guest editor in New York City, she fails to be accepted into a prestigious writing course and gradually loses much of her sanity and ambition. She mentally explores many wild scenarios for happiness and fulfillment (e.g., apprenticing herself to a pottery maker, finding a European lover), tries to write a novel, does such bizarre things as wearing her mother's clothes and eating raw meat, and finally attempts suicide. Obviously, she is not mentally well, but to some extent society's repressions for females and the lack of creative inspiration in her life have both contributed to her collapse.

Since society does not encourage Esther to excel—her excellent grades not withstanding—she sometimes competes in bizarre ways. For example, at a banquet for the guest interns at *Ladies' Day*, she eats ravenously as if she must consume more than any of the other interns. She also feels inferior to Buddy Willard because he lost his virginity before she did.

Topics for Further Study

- Explore some of the current career opportunities for females that did not exist in the 1950s.

- What are some of the circumstances that might lead a person to consider suicide? What are some indications that a person may be contemplating suicide? What can you do to intervene? Investigate the debate surrounding assisted suicide and argue one position.

- If a bright young person comes from a family without much money, how can that person improve his or her chances of obtaining a higher education? Is it better for that person to work full-time and put off college for a while or to work part-time and study part-time? Back up your opinion with some solid research.

Esther recovers much of her mental and emotional stability by the end of the novel, but the reasons for her improvement are not entirely clear. To some extent, Dr. Nolan has empowered Esther to understand her motivations, actions, and reactions, but some would argue Esther has at least partly responded to electroconvulsive shock. At least one critic, David Holbrook in *Sylvia Plath: Poetry and Existence*, even questions to what extent Esther has recovered, when he writes, "All that her therapy achieves is symbolised by the last chapter that blankets the asylum grounds ... Sylvia Plath's insight is not deceived. 'Treatment' merely freezes her." Linda Wagner-Martin disagrees: "... Esther has indeed entered a new phase ... she enters her new birth ritual, the process of leaving the asylum for the real world, with as much confidence as an intelligent person can muster ... There is no question that Plath intended to create a thoroughly positive ending for Esther's narrative." While the extent of Esther's recovery is debatable, the search for her identity will certainly continue after she is released from the asylum.

Point of View

Told in first person, Esther Greenwood narrates the entire novel *The Bell Jar*. From this perspective, the reader sees guest editor Esther in the miserable summer of 1953, her selective childhood and college memories, her romantic history, her breakdown and subsequent period of institutionalization, and her road to recovery. Despite her considerable intelligence, a careful reader will not necessarily take everything she says on faith, especially in light of her history of depression and occasionally bizarre behavior. The careful reader will also take into consideration that Esther's feelings shift quite abruptly on such subjects as role models and marriage. Though the narrative generally proceeds in a straightforward, chronological fashion, occasionally jumping back and forth in time, many questions arise. Why, for example, does Esther hate her mother so much? Why does she leave her drunken friend Doreen in the hotel hallway? Why does she reduce so many people around her to unpleasant stereotypes? Above all, why is Esther so unhappy? Part of the answer can be found in the oppressive 1950s environment, but can other factors figure into it? What factors really contributed to her recovery? After observing Esther in an assortment of situations, the reader can form his or her own impressions.

Setting

Literally, most of *The Bell Jar* takes place in either New York City or the Boston vicinity. The time is mostly the latter half of 1953, although Esther occasionally makes reference to earlier occasions in her narration. On a figurative level, much of the novel occurs in the mind of its protagonist, Esther Greenwood.

Symbolism

On the simplest level, *The Bell Jar*, Plath's only novel, refers to the social pressure for young women to marry in the 1950s. One of the causes of Esther's depression is her worry that she would not make a good wife for all of the following reasons: She cannot cook, stands too tall, and dances poorly. Unfortunately, she thinks her positive qualities—a high degree of intelligence, ambition, a literary aptitude—are actually handicaps in the marriage market. On other occasions, Esther thinks she could never be happy in any marriage, regardless of whom she finds as a husband.

The Bell Jar overflows with other symbolism; one of the most important is birth and rebirth. In one scene, Esther witnesses a birth in the teaching hospital where Buddy Willard works: "I was so struck by the sight of the table where they were lifting the woman I didn't say a word. It looked like some awful torture table, with these metal stirrups sticking up at mid-air at one end and all sorts of instruments and wires and tubes...." Her continuing description of the birthing is accurate and precise, but completely lacking in any sense of joy and wonderment. As Lynda K. Bundtzen writes in *Plath's Incarnations:* "The problem ... is that men have usurped the privilege of giving birth from women. The doctors are all male and they are entirely responsible for the emergence of a new creature into the world." So for Esther, a woman giving birth is no cause for celebration; it is symbolic of male oppression.

The subject of rebirth comes up figuratively in the conclusion of the novel. Note Esther's description of the elements: "The sun, emerged from its gray shrouds of clouds, shone with a summer brilliance on the untouched slopes ... I felt the profound thrill it gives me to see trees and grassland waist-high under flood water, as if the usual order of the world had shifted slightly, and entered a new phase."

Some critics have suggested that with the death of Joan Gilling, the character who most resembles Esther Greenwood, the latter is liberated from some of her pain. As Stan Smith notes in *Critical Quarterly*, "Esther is left wondering, at Joan's funeral, just what she thinks she is burying, the "wry black image" of her madness, or the 'beaming double of her old best self.' In a sense, the suicide of this surrogate is Esther's rebirth."

Absence of Feminism in the 1940s and 1950s

It is impossible to fully understand *The Bell Jar* without a realization of the relative absence of feminism in the United States in the 1940s and 1950s. Both decades were fairly prosperous ones in American history, and women's social and financial standing usually hung on their husbands' occupation and respective income. Although more than six million women went to work when America was engaged in World War II, after the war ended, many were encouraged to leave the work force. Dr. Benjamin Spock, who published the book *Baby and Child Care*, once even proposed that the federal government subsidize housewives to discourage them from entering into the work force. In *Modern Woman: The Lost Sex* (1946), authors Marynia Famham and Ferdinand Lundberg argued that women who worked sacrificed their essential femininity. While, of course, many single women worked out of economic necessity, they were not encouraged to show naked ambition or to stay in the work force indefinitely. A married woman—with or without children—who earned as much as her husband was rare.

Of course, women who worked in menial or low-paying jobs were less of a threat to mainstream

America. Hence, in *The Bell Jar*, Mrs. Greenwood encourages her daughter, Esther, to learn shorthand, because that skill will at least guarantee her some kind of job after college.

Compare & Contrast

- **1950s and 1960s:** As recently as 1950, men received approximately 76 percent of all degrees conferred in the United States. At the Master's level, men received roughly 2.5 times as many degrees as women.

  Today: In 1993, men received approximately 46 percent of all degrees conferred in the United States. Since 1986, women began receiving more Master's degrees than men, and the pattern continues.

- **1950s and 1960s:** In 1960, about 59 percent of single women were part of the American work force, about 32 percent of married women belonged to the work force, and about 42 percent of "other" (widowed, divorced, separated) women belonged to the work force.

  Today: In 1994, About 68 percent of single women were part of the American work force, about 61 percent of married women belonged to the work force, and about 48 percent of "other" (widowed, divorced, separated) women belonged to the work force.

- **1950s and 1960s:** The concept of date rape did not exist; if a woman went on a date with a man and was raped, she did not have any legal recourse.

  Today: Many more women are successfully suing men for date rape.

- **1950s and 1960s:** National Center for Health Statistics (NCHS) on suicide in America can never be entirely accurate or reliable, as many people who attempt or commit suicide often conceal their intention. Their families often conceal the suicide, too. However, NCHS statistics on suicides in 1953 reveal that men were more than three times as likely to commit suicide as women. White men in 1953 were more likely to commit suicide than any other racial/gender group; the second most likely group was nonwhite men; the third most likely group was white women; the least likely group was nonwhite women.

  Today: As of 1993, the racial/gender breakdown of 1953

had not changed; however, men are now about four times more likely to commit suicide than women.

In 1963, Betty Friedan's *The Feminine Mystique* was published. At the time, as in the 1950s, there were many more men in the work force and women earned far less money. However, this pivotal study of middle-class women's anger and some proposed solutions paved the way for a gradual redefinition of sex roles in America. In 1966, three years after Plath had taken her own life, Friedan and her colleagues established the National Organization for Women (NOW).

Mental Illness and Suicide

The Bell Jar is not simply about male oppression in the 1950s; it also tackles the topic of mental illness, although it does so in nonclinical terms. Specifically, it is about one depressed and confused woman's suicide attempt at a time when the medical profession often relied on such crude methods as electroconvulsive therapy (ECT). In ECT, a low electric charge is passed through a patient's body, to cure such illnesses as depression and schizophrenia. Like Esther in *The Bell Jar*, Sylvia Plath received ECT.

While many factors contribute to a person's choice in taking his or her own life, researchers have found that age, sex, and marital status are all statistically significant. For example, men are more likely to kill themselves than females today, although the opposite was true at the turn of the twentieth century. By the 1960s, there was some scientific evidence that married people were less suicideprone than single people; in turn, married people with children were not as likely to commit suicide as married or single people without children. To some extent, these statistics reflected the researcher's and society's biases. For example, Louis Dublin wrote in *Suicide: A Sociological and Statistical Study* that "the presence of children has a much greater saving effect on women than on men because the parental instinct is stronger among them." It is also important to remember that Sylvia Plath—a married (although also separated) woman with two young children—defied some of the statistical data. Finally, since there is a stigma about suicide, many families cover up the circumstances if a family member elects to take his or her own life. Hence, the official suicide statistics are not necessarily valid or reliable.

While such organizations as the National Save-a-Life League date back to 1906, the subject of suicide prevention remained shrouded in mystery for many American people for several decades. In 1958, the Suicide Prevention Center in Los Angeles began with a public grant from the U.S. Public Health Service. It was the first agency to use only professionals for its therapy sessions.

Critical Overview

Two years before Sylvia Plath published *The Bell Jar*, her collection of poetry *The Colossus* opened to some good reviews, particularly in the United States. That Plath published *The Colossus* under her own name but published *The Bell Jar* under the pseudonym of Victoria Lucas meant the reviewers would judge the latter on its own merits. Of course, the original critics of *The Bell Jar* did not know that its author was the estranged wife of Ted Hughes, who was becoming a successful poet in his own right.

Some early reviews were encouraging. Robert Taubman, in a *New Statesman* article, called *The Bell Jar* "a clever first novel.... The first feminine novel ... in the Salinger mood," referring to J.D. Salinger's famous novel *Catcher in the Rye* and some of his shorter work. Laurence Lerner in *The Listener* praised the book as "brilliant and moving," while Rupert Butler, in *Time and Tide*, found the book "terribly likeable" and "astonishingly skillful." All three critiques were published in January 1963, less than a month before Plath's suicide. By 1966, *The Bell Jar* had been published in England under Plath's real name.

Many latter reviews compared *The Bell Jar* to Plath's posthumous collection of poetry *Ariel.* C. B. Cox in a 1966 review for *Critical Quarterly* believed "the novel seems a first attempt to express mental states which eventually found a more appropriate form in poetry." However, Robert Scholes, writing for *The New York Times Book Review*, called *The Bell Jar* "a fine novel, as bitter and remorseless as her last poems." Like many other critics, he compared *The Bell Jar* to some of J. D. Salinger's work when he called the former "… the kind of book Salinger's Franny might have written about herself ten years later." (Franny is one of the fictional Glass children who appears in Salinger's *Franny and Zooey* as well as in some of his short stories.) M. L. Rosenthal wrote in the *Spectator* of the novel's "magnificent sections whose candour and revealed suffering will haunt anyone's memory."

Since its publication in 1963, *The Bell Jar* has steadily acquired a reputation as a feminist classic. In 1972, Patricia Meyer Spacks, in her *Hudson River* review, listed the ways in which the novel concerns female sexuality, "babies in glass jars, women bleeding in childbirth, Esther herself thrown in the mud by a sadist, hemorrhaging after a single sexual experience. To be a woman is to bleed and burn.…" Fourteen years later, Paula Bennett, in her book *My Life a Loaded Gun: Female Creativity and Feminist Politics*, perceived the novel as offering a brilliant evocation of "the oppressive atmosphere of the 1950s and the soul-destroying effect this atmosphere could have on ambitious, high-minded young women like Plath."

Although Sylvia Plath and her mother had feared publication of *The Bell Jar* in the United

States would embarrass many of the author's friends and acquaintances, much of the American reaction was mature. Some critics, including Ronald De Feo and Ruth Bauerle, defended the book as more than thinly veiled autobiography. It eventually became a Book-of-the-Month club selection, and *Book World* considered it one of the "Fifty Notable Books" of 1971.

In light of Plath's own suicide ten years after the time *The Bell Jar* actually took place, some readers and critics have found the novel's relatively optimistic conclusion to be unconvincing. Others, disagreeing, found it to be psychologically sound. For example, Tony Tanner in *City of Words: American Fiction, 1950-1970* believed the novel was "perhaps the most compelling and controlled account of a mental breakdown to have appeared in American fiction."

In retrospect, it must be stressed that Esther's problems in *The Bell Jar* aren't entirely typical of female teenagers' troubles today. As Susan Sniader Lanser and Teresa De Lauretis have written, Plath's work is about one woman in a specific period of American history when exciting career opportunities for women were rare. Esther's dilemma—marriage and children versus successful career—cannot be so easily generalized today. Also, while many male and female teenagers today face the difficult decision of whether to lose their virginity before marriage, few obsess over it to the point that Esther does in *The Bell Jar.*

Sources

Paula Bennett, *My Life a Loaded Gun*, Beacon, 1986.

Lynda K. Bundtzen, *"Women in The Bell Jar:* Two Allegories" from *Plath's Incamations: Women and the Creative Process*, University of Michigan Press, 1983.

Rupert Butler, "New American Fiction: Three Disappointing Novels—But One Good Time," in *Time and Tide*, January 31, 1963, p. 34.

C. B. Cox, editorial in *Critical Quarterly*, Autumn, 1966, p. 195.

Louis Dublin, *Suicide: A Sociological and Statistical Study*, Ronald, 1963.

David Holbrook, *Sylvia Plath: Poetry and Existence*, Athlone, 1976.

Laurence Lerner, "New Novels," in *Listener*, January 31, 1963, p. 215.

M. L. Rosenthal, "Blood and Plunder," in *Spectator*, September 30, 1966, p. 418.

Robert Scholes, review in *New York Times Book Review*, April 11, 1971, p. 7.

Stan Smith, "Attitudes Counterfeiting Life: The Irony of Artifice in Sylvia Plath's *The Bell Jar,"* in *Critical Quarterly*, Autumn, 1975, pp. 247–60.

Patricia Meyer Spacks, "A Chronicle of Women," in

Hudson River, Spring, 1972, p. 164.

Tony Tanner, in his *City of Words: American Fiction, 1950–1970*, Harper & Row, 1971.

Robert Taubman, "Anti-heroes," *New Statesman*, January 25, 1963, pp. 127–28.

Linda Wagner-Martin, *The Bell Jar: A Novel of the Fifties*, Twayne, 1992.

For Further Study

Paul Alexander, editor, *Ariel Ascending: Writings about Sylvia Plath*, Harper, 1985.

> One of the first anthologies of critical essays on Plath which, overall, focus more on her literary accomplishments than on the details of her life.

Ruth Bauerle, "Plath, at Last," in *Plain Dealer*, April 25, 1971, p. H7.

> Argues that the novel is more than an autobiographical success.

Elaine Connell, *Sylvia Plath: Killing the Angel in the House*, Pennine Pens, 1993.

> A brief but competent guide to Plath's biography and her critical history, combined with some uncomplicated interpretations of Plath's works, including *The Bell Jar.*

Ronald De Feo, review in *Modern Occasions*, Fall, 1971, pp. 624–25.

> Published shortly after the novel was published in the United States, this critique perceives the novel as more than a cult classic, praising it for qualities unrelated to its

autobiographical elements.

Teresa De Lauretis, "Rebirth in the Bell Jar," in *Women's Studies*, 3 (1975), pp. 173–83.

Article suggests *The Bell Jar* must be viewed be in terms of a historical perspective.

Marynia Farmham and Ferdinand Lundberg, *Modern Woman: The Lost Sex*, Harper, 1947.

Authors make the case for women not being in the work force.

Betty Friedan, *The Feminine Mystique*, Norton, 1963.

Pivotal study of middle-class, American women's dissatisfaction with sex roles.

Susan Sniader Lanser, "Beyond *The Bell Jar:* Women Students of the 1970s," in *Radical Teacher*, December, 1977, pp. 41–4.

Article stresses that Plath's novel must be viewed in the context of the 1950s.

Sheryl L. Meyering, *Sylvia Plath: A Reference Guide, 1973–1988*, G. K. Hall, 1990.

An extensive bibliography of Plath criticism up to 1988.

Charles Newman, editor, *The Art of Sylvia Plath: A Symposium*, Indiana University Press, 1970.

An early assortment of reviews,

reminiscences, thenunpublished poems, and critical essays. Some of the essays are uniquely analytical in their approach to Plath's poetry. Includes a brief essay on *The Bell Jar* written before the novel had been published in the United States.

Sylvia Plath, *Collected Poems*, edited by Ted Hughes, Harper, 1981.

Plath's complete poems, including juvenilia, with notes by Hughes. Winner of the 1982 Pulitzer Prize.

Sylvia Plath, *The Journals of Sylvia Plath*, edited by Ted Hughes and Frances McCullough, Dial Press, 1982.

Selections from Plath's private journals.

Aurelia Schober Plath, editor, *Letters Home: Correspondence 1950–1963*, Harper, 1975.

A collection of Plath's letters edited by her mother.

Ellen Rosenberg, "Sylvia Plath," in *Concise Dictionary of American Literary Biography: The New Consciousness, 1941–1968*, edited by Richard Layman and Lucia Tarbox, Gale Research Company, 1987, pp. 408–22.

Provides biographical information on Sylvia Plath, as well as some analysis of her poetry.

Jacqueline Rose, *The Haunting of Sylvia Plath*, Virago Press, 1991.

> Focusing primarily on Plath's poetry, Rose promotes the term "fantasy" as a key term by which to understand the complexities of Plath's self-representation and her psychologized, gendered, and sexualized poetics.

Toni Salvidar, *Sylvia Plath: Confessing the Fictive Self* Lang, 1992.

> In a study primarily of Plath's poetry, Salvidar takes issue with those who reject the "confessional" label for Plath. She argues that Plath asserts a fictive "r" by presenting selective incidents from her life in order to incarnate a real, individual self through literature.

Anne Stevenson, *Bitter Fame: A Life of Sylvia Plath*, Viking, 1989.

> Of the many Plath biographies, Stevenson's is perhaps the least speculative. It received considerable blessing from the Hughes estate, which controls Plath's writings.

Linda W. Wagner, editor, *Critical Essays on Sylvia Plath*, G. K. Hall, 1984.

> A collection of reviews and critical essays, the latter mostly written from

a feminist literary perspective.

Linda W. Wagner, editor, *Sylvia Plath: The Critical Heritage*, Routledge, 1988.

> A valuable anthology of reviews and short studies of Plath's work. Includes short biographical information on the reviewers.

CPSIA information can be obtained
at www.ICGtesting.com
Printed in the USA
BVHW091022011118
531819BV00018B/541/P